YOGA REVOLUTION:

HOW YOGA WILL TRANSFORM AMERICA

by Michael R. McBrearty

"The whole of history is nothing but a continual
transformation of human nature."
(Karl Marx, *The Poverty of Philosophy*)

dedicated to my brother, John McBrearty (1948-2012)

CONTENTS

1.
WE DON'T UNDERSTAND
HOW YOGA WILL CHANGE US

Growing with the 21st century, our society has witnessed the rise of mass Yoga practice. In 2004, three million Americans practiced Yoga at least twice a week. By 2007, "more than ten million people said they had practiced yoga" (1). By 2010, the number of Americans doing Yoga had surpassed 14 million. More recently, *The New York Times* reported that "some estimate as many as 20 million" practice today. And, if history is any guide, the arrival of Yoga will, in the long run, radically change the U.S.

It is not an Orientalist cliché, but an historic fact. As Western industrialization is rapidly transforming the material life of China and India, at the same time, Eastern mysticism is slowly transforming the mental life of the U.S. As organized religion declines, "spirituality" advances. We Americans are discovering a new, New World—the world within. After a long time, we will acquire knowledge of that world and its powers.

Experience in all countries of the earth has shown that one cannot possibly cultivate a spiritual life without at the same time calling forth psychic powers . . . . This fact can cause astonishment only where spiritual practices are virtually unknown. (2)

Yet there is little understanding of how this slow-motion, tidal wave of mystical knowledge will, in the long run, inundate U.S. society. And that includes those blithely surfing this giant wave—those now practicing Yoga.

First of all, Americans do not grasp that doing Yoga causes Enlightenment, that is, a *permanently, radically altered, state of consciousness.* In fact, most of those practicing Yoga don't think they will reach Enlightenment (also called Realization or Liberation). They picture it as a far-off state of perfection. They mis-identify Enlightenment with the Western concept of Sainthood, a status that is extraordinarily rare.

The sages of the East have a different view. Of course, you must first learn to discipline the mind. To acquire that ability takes not years but *decades* of daily, regular effort. But then you *do* reach the goal of Realization. It is the normal and expected outcome of Yoga practice.

In Hinduism, the Tantric Yogis in particular emphasize that, in this very lifetime, it is a practical, realizable goal. In Tantrism, "Enlightenment or Self-Realization is not an otherworldly experience. It is here and now." (3) The Indian Buddhist scripture the *Dhammapada* (the Path of Virtue) asserts, "In this very life (on earth) /One may reach insight supreme." (4)

In Japan, the famous monk Esai wrote of Zen meditation, "By practicing it, one attains Enlightenment in the span of this life." (5) In both traditions, to practice meditation and Yoga without reaching Liberation would be as pointless as taking a trip without reaching the destination.

Americans also don't comprehend—yet—how totally transforming an experience Enlightenment consciousness actually is. For this is the mind-set in general of our conservative society.

We are taught that expectations of radical change, personal or political, are unrealistic. As the Marxist critic Raymond Williams wrote, after World War II, there came to prevail, in both Britain and America, "an orthodox . . . mood in which all humane and positive beliefs, especially a belief in radical change, were recognized in advance either as a projection of some personal or social maladjustment, or as an inexperienced, naïve, adolescent idealism" (6). The idea that one could bring about radical change is seen as not only wrong or mistaken but as irrational and crazy.

Yoga as a process, by contrast, demonstrates a faith in a doctrine that is truly revolutionary. That is the dialectical law of the transformation of quantity into quality. (7) Yoga is exactly such a process--where enough long-term *quantity* yields an explosive, radical change in *quality.* The quantity, in this case, is the period of years of repetitive practice or "sadhana."

The drastic change in quality which results is called Enlightenment. It is a process within the individual that is not reformist but revolutionary. It is what Marxists call a "rapid leap"—a revolutionary break. There is no more radical personality change.

In her history of Western mysticism, Evelyn Underhill specified a metaphor used for centuries by medieval Europeans to describe how a person was changed by mystical work. It was the transformation of iron. When heated in a furnace the metal changes from a cold, dark, solid into a white-hot liquid. It was the most drastic image of change their society knew. (8)

In years to come, thousands of Americans, previously inert, will reach the white-hot state of Enlightenment. They will have radically transformed their minds. Their powerful, cosmic world-outlook will be utterly at odds with the present individualistic, competitive society. Their values will be so contrary to the *status quo* that they will have no choice but to become a counter-culture.

At that point what began as merely an exotic alternative health trend will become a powerful society within our society and then a revolutionary political movement. (Note the daily Yoga classes at the Occupy Wall Street sites--now violently repressed--yet the first fruits.)

Could those believing in the current system, welcoming mind-altering Yogic ways, be as naive as those Native Americans who canoed out to welcome the ships of the Europeans, whose superior technical knowledge proved so disastrous to them? If the comparison sounds far fetched, consider the spread of Buddhism over all Asia.

There, Buddhism was the vehicle for transmitting knowledge of meditation and Yoga practices, as Hatha Yoga, the physical exercises, are merely the vehicle for the knowledge in the US today. It takes time and social practice for any culture to, in Marx's phrase, "discover the rational kernel within the mystical shell:" (9)

A historian of Buddhism described how this process of discovery took place in China:

> When the Chinese were first brought face to face with Indian Buddhism with its rich and elaborate imagery, concepts, and modes of thinking, they were fascinated at first and finally overwhelmed and conquered. After a few centuries, however, the practical nature of the Chinese began asserting itself; it began to search for certain features within Buddhism which it could understand and practice, and in this search it soon picked out the *dhyana* [meditation] exercise as the essence of Buddhist discipline. (10)

2.
GUATAMA BUDDHA AND V.I. LENIN

The transforming social effect of Yoga knowledge on ancient Asia society is evident from a consideration of the life of Buddha--looked at not from the usual religious angle, but from an historical point of view. The Enlightened One's career of preaching and organizing was in fact a response to the social crisis of his time.

The first accounts of the founder of Buddhism were not written down until five centuries after his death. For pious reasons, legendary exaggerations were included. Buddha's father, for example, was depicted as having been a nation-ruling king. We do know, however, that Guatama, advocate of non-violence, was born not a Brahmin priest but a member of the warrior caste. His clan, the Sakyas, ruled an area at the foot of the Himalayan mountains in what is now Nepal. Historians call the form of its government, with freely elected rulers, a "tribal republic."

The c. 500 BC North Indian society that produced the Buddha was, as the Indian Marxist scholar Debiprasad Chattopadhyaya observed, an era of "colossal social upheavals." (11) The rising kingdom-states of the Ganges plain, with their international trade and rich cities, were destroying the surviving peripheral tribal societies like Buddha's and exterminating their populations. A ruthless king of one of the new states massacred many of Buddha's own tribe.

Engels wrote about the identical transformation of Athenian society from tribal government to city-states in classical times. Society was changing completely:

> from an organization of tribes for the free administration of their own affairs it was transformed into an organization for plundering and oppressing their neighbors; and correspondingly its organs were transformed from instruments of the will of the people into the independent organs for ruling and oppressing their own people. (12)

This change, from tribes based on kinship and common ownership, to kingdoms based on class and exploitation, was taking place in other areas around the globe. It brought forth new teachers like Buddha, Socrates and the Hebrew Prophets. It was made possible by the invention of a powerful new medium—the alphabet. As an historian of languages noted, "The political effects of this were massive." (13) Media theorist Marshall McLuhan described the impact of this ancient media change-over:

> The alphabet meant power and authority and control of military structures at a distance. . . . The alphabet spelled the end of the stationary temple bureaucracies and the priestly monopolies of

knowledge and power. Unlike pre-alphabetic writing, which with its innumerable signs was difficult to master . . . . . the easier alphabet . . . effected the transfer of power from the priestly to the military caste. (14)

***

Characteristically, in an age when philosophical texts were written in Sanskrit, Buddha urged his disciples to instead use the vernacular language of the people to get the message across. (15) In his biographies, like many heroes of religion, Buddha was depicted as fleeing a life of utter sensual enjoyment (at a royal court) to one of complete religious asceticism (in the wilderness).

Unlike many Eastern sages, however, he returned to society with a practical solution for society's problems.

Indian religion, in Buddha's time, was owned and operated by the Brahmin class of priests. Their scriptures, the *Vedas*, the most ancient in the world, composed perhaps 1500 BC, were considered inerrant. The Brahmins monopolized mystical knowledge. Society and nature itself were thought to depend on their ritual sacrifices to the gods.

By contrast, Buddha's quest for Enlightenment, which took six hard years of full-time Yoga meditation, did not at any point involve any imagined god or supernatural force. Through his own *human* effort alone, Guatama became the Buddha ("Enlightened One"). As a twentieth century Buddhist has written:

For the first time in history, he gave men the power to think for themselves, raised the worth of mankind and showed that man can reach to the highest knowledge and supreme Enlightenment by his own efforts. (16)

Soon after achieving his goal, Buddha felt an urge to share his insight with others. But when he considered his own extreme difficulty in obtaining Enlightenment--and the mindset of the average, busy, sensual woman or man— Buddha came to a conclusion that demonstrates his psychological realism. He concluded that it would be useless!

Legend has it that a god from heaven had to tell Buddha that there were *some* people who he, Buddha, would be able to awaken from ignorance. So he became history's first and most successful proselytizing propagandist. How did he succeed?

First, his solution was personal (the "Buddha"). He was his own best example of the truth of his ideas. He himself, with his charismatic powers and compassionate "Buddha nature," personified a selfless, liberated individual. For forty-five years, Buddha appeared in one Indian city after another, like a pop star on an endless tour.. Tradition states he did not spend a single day of those forty-five years without teaching and explaining his way of relieving human suffering. (17)

Secondly, his solution was ideological (the "Dharma"). He taught the correct theory or Dharma, including the techniques or meditation methods that actually led to Enlightenment (then as now, these physical/psychological practices really did totally transform consciousness).

Philosophically, in opposition to the Brahmin's Vedic notion of an eternal, unchanging, inner Self ("Atman"), Buddha posited revolutionary views: the ideas of universal impermanence ("Anityata-vada") and no permanent soul ("Anatama-vada"). They were, as the Marxist historian Chattopadhyaya noted, "the first instance of dialectical thinking in Indian philosophy." (18)

Thirdly, and most importantly, his solution was organizational (the "Sangha"). He did not try to convert everyone. He knew that only a minority would understand his teaching. So he did not build a mass organization, which anyone could join. Instead, his followers were a vanguard of trained cadres.

He organized his disciples into the first monastic order or "sangha." The monks were not part time householders, but full-time activists, like Lenin's Vanguard Party, made up of full-time revolutionaries.

Both social innovators, Buddha and Lenin, understood that, as Lenin put it, "no revolutionary movement can endure without a stable organization of leaders maintaining continuity." (19) As described in his book, *What Is To Be Done?,* Lenin's party was organized around putting out a national newspaper (first *Iskra,* then *Pravda*). (20) Similarly, Buddha's sangha was organized around the main medium of his time: oratory, in the daily sermon.

Note that using this medium retained the old, oral ways of the vanishing tribal society. Buddha himself wrote nothing. His sayings, when written down centuries later, tend to begin with the formula, "This I heard." The rules of the order (the *vinaya*) too were not written down but recited by the community of monks monthly.

Buddhism made a special study of what were called skillful means (*Upaya kasusalya*) in teaching. The ideal was to teach what your listeners, whether farmers, merchants or scholars, had the capacity to understand, depending on their intellectual level. Instead of recluses meditating in caves, the role of the monks was to explain the Dharma to the lay public. They were propagandists for the new meditation-based way of life. (Recent events in Asia show Buddhist monks still strongly influencing society, for good and ill.)

In our epoch, Lenin similarly understood that, left to themselves, the workers, absorbed in economic struggles, could develop at best a trade union mentality. Within the capitalist system, we workers are, as Rosa Luxemburg put it, condemned to the labors of Sisyphus, pre-occupied with just fighting off the attacks of the bosses.

To raise the workers' consciousness beyond the day-by-day, economic struggle to a revolutionary level would take knowledge coming from outside the closed system. As Lenin said, "Class political consciousness can be brought to the workers *only from outside"* (21).

What Marxism sees on a social level, Buddhism depicts on a cosmic level. Marx depicts the Satanic mill of capitalist society as a Moloch grinding up the workers, driven by the universal force of greed. In, Buddhism, similarly, the universal driving forces are greed and desire (which is a kind of greed) and anger (a reaction to greed frustrated).

Like the workers enslaved by capitalism, Buddhism depicts humankind as hopelessly caught up in the wheel of life and death and suffering. Blinded by ignorance, we re-incarnate again and again. Within this system, there is no way out. That is why in *mandalas* or schematic diagrams of the universe, Buddha is always depicted as outside and above the wheel. Like his fellow innovator Lenin, Buddha believed the liberating Dharma had to come from *outside* the infernal system.

For Buddha knew that, in the real world, householders, concerned by necessity with supporting their families and trying to survive, had little chance for meditation. However, they shared in the moral merit earned by the good *karma* (action) of the monks by supporting them.

This mutual interaction--of monks teaching laymen compassionate ethics and laymen supporting monks--set the social pattern for much of Asia and beyond. "Throughout Buddhist history, the laity as individuals and communities has supported the Sangha in return for its instruction and guidance in the fundamental meaning of life." (22)

In addition, Buddha's order of monks reproduced the fraternity of the tribal republics--which were being destroyed--in their internal organization:

> Buddha did not look forward to . . . the rising state powers. Instead, he looked backward to the tribal collectives . . . . Apparently, he was pleading for a moral reform of the world . . . . The Buddha could clearly see the futility of practicing all these [right values] in the society at large. So he asked the people . . . "to go out" of the actual society and "to arrive at" the life of the *sangha* or the order of the monks. For within the *sangha*, things were different. Modeled consciously on the tribal collectives—without private property and with full equality and democracy among the brethren . . . The *sanghas* [became] classless societies within the bosom of the class society . . . . (23)

In the hyper-Jim Crow world of fifth century BC India, it was a tremendous social advance that people of any caste could join the order and achieve Enlightenment. The magical monopoly of the pale, Brahmin priest-caste was broken. "It is not birth but deeds that makes a Brahmin," the Buddhist scripture said. (24)

The admittance of women (again of any caste shade) into a separate order of nuns was also a giant step forward for those times. Women who had attained Enlightenment were among the Buddha's leading disciples. (25)

The number of followers of Buddha's way grew

steadily. But for the first two centuries they were confined to the Ganges Valley. Ironically, Buddhism, the way of non-violence, formed in reaction to the rise of warring Kings, became a world religion only after being taken up by just such a King, the empire-founding Asoka (c. 270-230 BC).

Born ruler of a North Indian state, he waged a series of wars that for the first time politically united almost all of the vast Indian sub-continent. Unlike the Roman Emperor Constantine, who made Christianity the religion of Rome because he believed it helped him achieve military victory, the Emperor Asoka converted to Buddhism out of remorse for the violence his conquests had made necessary. He proclaimed as his first principle of government *ahimsa* or non-harmfulness.

Remembered for millennia as the archetypal "good king" (the wheel of Dharma, his symbol, adorns the flag of India today), besides his massive secular public works like roads and canals, to promote Buddhism, the Emperor Asoka founded many monasteries, held a universal church council and sent out missionaries in four directions. Buddhism made use of political unity to become the official ideology of India.

3.
HOW BUDDHISM CONQUERED CHINA

Then Buddhism just as successfully made use of political *dis*-unity to achieve ideological hegemony in China. In 220 AD, the empire of the Han Dynasty, which had unified China, collapsed--along with the credibility of its ruling, familial, Confucian ideology. "When the Han fell, Confucianism was utterly discredited." (26)

For several centuries thereafter China was divided. Barbarian invaders overran the old heartland of Northern China and established new dynasties. The aristocrats who could, escaped to southern China, then a sparsely populated frontier region, where a weaker, Chinese-ruled state held on. But the catastrophe demoralized the exiled grandees. Having lost their old world, Buddhism appealed to them as a philosophy that rationalized impermanence.

In the North, at the same time, Buddhism was supported by new rulers precisely because it was a world-view that was in origin, like they were, non-Chinese. Missionary monks from Central Asia or the Southern kingdom proved able political and military advisers to these rulers as well as impressive, shaman-like, miracle makers.

"The amazing thing was that in spite of many features within Buddhism which were opposed to Chinese culture, the religion was still able to win the . . . adherence of the Chinese." (27) As conservative Confucians charged, by encouraging people to leave society and enter monasteries, Buddhism destroyed traditional Chinese family values. They also argued that Buddhism was not Chinese in origin and therefore "barbaric."

At the various Imperial Courts, the "Chinese officials, striving always . . . to reconstitute a Confucian state in which the educated gentry would have the key role" (28), engaged in a centuries-long culture war against the new Buddhist ideas. They "wanted to recreate the ideal feudal society so highly praised by Confucius, where the literati held all the power and where the masses of people remained ignorant but pledged loyalty to the rulers." (29)

In contrast to the reactionary mandarins, for part of each year the Buddhist monks left their monasteries and preached the Dharma in the countryside to the peasants. The monks used lectures, debates and, in particular, vivid storytelling, to get across basic moral teachings of compassion and nonviolence to their unlearned audiences. "Those who embraced Buddhism were mostly of peasant stock." (30)

For literate urban laymen, they set up religious societies to study the *sutras*, aphoristic wisdom texts. The monks' efforts in this line were much facilitated by the invention in China of paper (made from textiles) to mass produce block-printed books. Printed designs of *Mandalas* or magical diagrams were also popular. As the pioneering historian of media, Harold Innis, wrote, "Printing emerged from the demands of Buddhism in its appeal to the masses," further noting that, "Access to supplies of paper in China enabled Buddhists to develop block printing on a large scale." (31)

Employing this new medium , the monks worked to propagandize a popular, devotional form of Buddhism which gradually took hold of the Chinese population.

Besides instructing them, the Buddhists won over the people by working zealously to improve their material conditions. Monks established hospitals, old age homes and orphanages. They assisted community projects like digging wells and building roads.

The States entrusted them with storing reserves of grain to be distributed to the peasants in times of famine. The monks provided a kind of work release program: prisoners who promised to reform were released to work for the monastery. On holidays, great vegetarian feasts were given in temples that attracted both nobles and crowd of commoners who were pointedly served as equals.

In 590 AD, Emperor Wen-Ti conquered the Southern states and re-united China. In conscious imitation of Emperor Asoka, he proclaimed Buddhism the state religion, founded monasteries and sent out missionaries. He was thus acknowledging the reality that Buddhism had, during the period of disunity, become the world-view of the Chinese masses and many of their rulers as well. (32)

In the long run, the monasteries grew wealthy, exploited peasants, and were suppressed [c.849] and their wealth seized by the Emperor.

As the Indian historian Chattopadhyaya concluded, of Buddhism's original "grandeur," that

> Because Buddha was drawing so much from preclass [that is, tribal] society, Buddhism, at least in its early phase, both in organization and ideology, was remarkably free from the characteristic illusions of class society . . . .

Nevertheless, he first admitted the creed's limitation:

> Rather than effecting a real social revolution, Buddhism eventually passed into its opposite . . . and served the people as a palliative [ineffective remedy] for the very iniquities which it originally wanted to fight. (33)

(It seems there is a recurrent dialectical course of history, for countercultures--monastic religious movements and, later, revolutionary political parties, alike. First, they succeed in recruiting members and support because of their ascetic, militant opposition to dominant cultural values. Then, this very success brings power and wealth, attracts cynical opportunists--and their worldliness and corruption discredits and ruins the movement. After their fall, new, militant orders or parties, in turn, arise and replace them.

(So there is a half-truth in Eric Hoffer's crack,

"Every great cause begins as a movement, becomes a business and eventually degenerates into a racket." What Hoffer missed is the other half of the social motion, that is, when the people get wise to the racketeers, throw them out and start new and true radical movements.)

In any case, from India and China, across Asia, to Bhutan, Tibet, Mongolia, Sri Lanka, Korea, Japan, and what are now Burma, Thailand, Laos and Vietnam—the story was the same. What had been, in each nation, a foreign, alien religion, became so intertwined with the culture as to be eventually considered central to it. Each country was ideologically conquered.

Each in its own way transformed Buddhism to meet its own historic needs and, in return, each society was radically changed by the introduction of Yoga meditation knowledge. (34) There is no reason to think that the same process will not take place in America in the decades to come.

4.
YOGA IN AMERICA

Under such unlikely and typically American guises as books advocating Zen meditation for career success and instructional Yoga tapes for weight loss, a grass-roots acquisition of mystical techniques is taking place in America today. It is a slow, from-the-ground-up process of mass education. Nevertheless, in the long run, the new knowledge will carry the day, just as in India and China.

The most important reason is simply that Yogic techniques actually *work*. That is why Buddhism appealed to the practical Chinese. As a Chinese Buddhist, Nan Huai-Chin, explained, "Buddhism . . . offered methods for genuine realization of spiritual powers and meditative concentration that could be relied on, in actual fact."

Indeed, the social impact of Yoga and meditation knowledge spreading to average Americans may change our society more fundamentally than any Oriental culture.

Consider that in Asia, Buddhist monks, though interacting through alms-collecting and preaching, lived, like the Hindu sages, apart from the people. But mystics in

America will be householders in the midst of society. This is a social fact without precedent. "For millenniums, the only people who practiced every day were monks . . . 'The way that its practiced now in daily life is quite new,'" a Yoga scholar declared recently. (35)

Transforming as they were, nevertheless the Buddhist cultural revolutions of Asia, in the final analysis, changed only those in the literate classes. For the Chinese masses, for example, worship of Buddha simply joined the worship of Taoist and folk gods. The hard-pressed peasants had little time for meditation. "Ultimately Buddhist, Taoist and folk-religious elements fused into an almost undifferentiated popular religion." (36)

In America today, however, genuine Realization-reaching techniques are becoming available to millions of ordinary people. Marx wrote that, "theory also becomes a material force once it has gripped the masses". (37) Mass Yoga Enlightenment will become a political force. For the first time anywhere in the history of the world, the US working class will take on as its task the "Great Work" of inner transformation.

In years past, rightly sensing a mortal threat to their ideological dominance over America, conservative Christians succeeded in banning the teaching of meditation techniques in schools. In 1997, in New Jersey, in the case of *Malnak versus Maharishi Mahesh Yogi*, a Federal District Court ruled that Transcendental Meditation is "religious in nature" and therefore that the teaching of TM in the public schools violated the first amendment of the U.S. Constitution. (38)

Now, the Transcendental Meditation movement is explicitly secular, boasting of having taught *mantras* to priests, rabbis and atheists. The TM movement has funded many scientific studies attempting to verify the *mantras'* beneficial effects. (39)

Nevertheless, the judge prohibited public money from being spent to teach Transcendental Meditation. His rationale was that such instruction would promote the worship of Shiva and Vishnu. (Logically, he should have gone ahead and banned public school teaching of Greek philosophy as promoting the worship of Zeus and Apollo.) And conservative Christians have worked to keep education about Yoga *asanas* out of schools as well.

However this exclusion will be increasingly challenged. In a sign of how attitudes have changed, consider the 2013 court case over a plan to teach Yoga postures as Physical Education in the public schools of Encinitas, California. The planned instructions were completely secular. No religious references of any kind were permitted. Despite this, in a law suit, local Christian parents charged that the Yoga courses violated the state's constitutional principle of the separation of church and state.

Unlike in 1997, in 2013, the California court ruled that teaching Yoga was *not* teaching religion--and gave the school district permission to go ahead. The Christian parents have appealed the decision. According to journalist Stewart J. Lawrence, they could eventually fight the decision, or others like it, all the way to the Supreme Court.

(40)

Fear is their weapon. Reactionary clergy try to make people afraid of acquiring Yoga knowledge. With typical, Western arrogance, these pseudo-educated preachers slander Oriental religions, thousands of years older than their Bible, as "demonic." (41) One of their sites warns, "Christians practicing yoga need to cease immediately, repent of it, and asks God's forgiveness."

Such fear-mongering will not succeed. Americans are pragmatists. They may be frightened of the preacher's Hellfire. But, in the end, the freedom of the wonderful states of consciousness that anyone can reach by these ancient Asian ways will overcome their fear. In the end, they will reach, not fearful submission to the Lord (which in practice, means submission to the their fundamentalist preacher) but a powerful self-mastery.

After all, Americans have had a mania for self-improvement since the early days of the Republic. The first self-made nation has always produced self-made persons. Classics like the autobiographies of Benjamin Franklin or Frederick Douglass, or Henry Thoreau's *Walden Pond* or Walt Whitman's *Song of Myself*--or the middlebrow self-help works of Dale Carnegie or Napoleon Hill--or whatever book in that category is currently a best seller—all testify (on different cultural levels) to this characteristic national obsession.

At the same time, self-developmental work has been for millennia absolutely central to Asian ways of wisdom. As a Buddhist scripture says, "Engineers channel water . . .

carpenters carve wood, wise people mold (discipline) themselves." (42) Conversely, in the land of fierce Zen self cultivation, in the modernizing nineteenth century, the archetypal work in this category, Samuel Smiles' *Self Help*, a bestseller in Britain and the US, reportedly sold one million copies in Japan. (43)

Transformative Asian practices and the American love for self-help routines were made for each other. So Yoga's U.S. popularity should be no surprise: it is the ultimate self-improvement program. "Yoga is the perfect practical system of self culture." (Swami Sivananda) (44)

***

The political impact which mass Yoga practice will have will be the result of a decidedly *long term* process. Long-term trends can take decades to reveal themselves.

Many now confidently assert that they are just into Yoga for the physical benefits, not the world view. They will one day seem as naive as the old advertisements featuring scientific-looking Doctors endorsing the health benefits of Camels. (45) As surely as tobacco causes deadly cancer, in the long run, Yoga causes blissful Enlightenment. But most Americans who practice Yoga have been doing so for only a few years. And to reach Enlightenment normally takes decades.

That is one reason why Swamis and monks are honored in the East. Their altered states of consciousness are recognized as being the product of long, sustained effort. As Swami Sivananda wrote, "Success comes in

Yoga after a long time. . . . . Be always patient and persevering." (46) The same advice was given by Swami Vivekenanda: "Nothing is done in a day . . . . It requires hard and constant practice. The mind can be conquered only by slow and steady practice." (47)

Americans by contrast want instant gratification. We want to get Enlightenment in thirty days. The attitude is, If it's real, shouldn't we be able to get it *now?*

And in terms of our society, with its ever-changing technology, this is a completely realistic attitude. If you spent thirty years learning a skill in America, by the time you mastered the technique, it would be obsolete. But the technology of Enlightenment is based on the physical human body/mind and that does not change quickly. The permanently altered state of consciousness is not a rookie of the year, but rather a lifetime achievement, award.

Thus the social effects of mass Yoga practice will take decades to be revealed.

5.
YOGA FOR SALE?

Besides *time*, another factor obscuring the coming political impact of mass Yoga practice is *money*—that is, the commercialization of Yoga. Once, Asian mystical ideas explicitly challenged selfish bourgeois values and the capitalist system. In October 1967, for example, tens of thousands of anti-War protestors surrounded the Pentagon, chanting demon-destroying mantras. (48)

Along with psychedelic drugs and revolutionary Marxism, Eastern mysticism was recognized as a primary ingredient of the 1960s revolutionary counter-culture. "In the sixties . . . The young were promiscuously drawn to both Marx and the occult, Mao and the *I Ching,* politics and pot, revolution and rock." (49)

Today, by contrast, Yoga seems to have been assimilated into the dominant system. Real, ascetic sages from India are passé. Since the 1990's, big corporations have offered their employees Yoga lessons as a corporate perk. Teaching postures or "asanas" has become a multi-billion dollar business. "In 2004 . . . Americans spent $2.95

billion on yoga classes, yoga-related products like clothing, books and mats, and on yoga retreats and vacations . . . Yoga has . . . become a fashionable lifestyle pursuit . . . . Yoga is growing fastest within the 18-to-24-year-old group." (50) By 2012, the Yoga industry had grown to a $6 billion dollar a year industry.

One company alone, Yoga-works of California, has a chain of fourteen "studios" across the country. To meet the great demand for classes, they are expanding as rapidly as possible. "Its almost like yoga studios are becoming like Starbucks," commented one instructor. By 2005, some 70,000 people had gotten certified as yoga teachers.

Enlightenment is on sale, the New Age industry promises. With incredible vulgarity, mystical knowledge is marketed like any other commodity. Want real metaphysical insight? Just buy our metaphysical book or DVD or lecture. In other words, the usual capitalist swindle. As an Apostle complained, of the false teachers of his day, "They think that religion is a way to grow rich." (1 Timothy 6:5)

But such commercialization is futile and self-contradictory. Enlightenment is about self-transformation not capitalist self-seeking. Augmenting the ego, competing to be number one, is the opposite process from Realization. To make your mind infinite, you have to destroy your ego.

Enlightenment is the psychological equivalent of an atomic explosion. Just as splitting the atom releases nuclear energy, so splitting the ego releases Enlightenment. You must destroy your individual ego (matter), in order to release your portion of the infinite mind (energy). As Swami Sivananda wrote, "When the vessel is broken, its light appears without." (51)

On the other hand, the greedy capitalist drive for individual success is the 180-degree opposite of the self-effacing process medieval mystics called "self-naughting." It is not a question of morality. It is simply psychologically impossible to serve both mysticism and Mammon.

Nevertheless, in the long run, major social change will result, from the current mass marketing of Yoga. This is despite the fact that the motives of the individuals spreading Yogi knowledge may be purely commercial!

This is not contradictory but rather the usual course of historical events. It is normal that vast social changes are promoted unconsciously by persons motivated simply by desire for gain. As Friedrich Engels put it, "Naked greed has been the moving spirit of civilization from the first day of its existence to the present time." (52)

At the end of feudal times, for example, when kings and nobles still ruled, the merchants went beyond at-home, small–scale production and began to set up large workshops or "manufactories." These early capitalists weren't consciously trying to start a process that would end in the French Revolution overthrowing the rule of the noble class. In the end, the rise to power of the bourgeoisie did just that. But each individual businessman just wanted to make more profits.

In another ironic example, it was businessmen

seeking profits in Russia who created a Russian working class or proletariat of industrial workers who then proceeded to partner with the farmers and throw the bourgeoisie out of power in the October 1917 Revolution.

The authors of an official history of the Soviet Communist Party, published in 1938, noted this historical paradox:

> When the Russian capitalists . . . implanted modern large-scale machine industry in Russia . . . they, of course, did not know and did not stop to reflect what *social* consequences this extensive growth of productive forces would lead to, they did not realize or understand that this big leap . . . would lead to a regrouping of social forces that would enable the proletariat to effect a union with the peasantry and to bring about a victorious Socialist revolution. They simply wanted . . . to squeeze as much profit as possible out of the national economy.
>
> (*The Short Course*) (53)

6.
ENLIGHTENMENT IS REVOLUTIONARY

Now, of those millions of Americans currently practicing Yoga, how many will acquire the revolutionary new viewpoint of Enlightenment?

Jesus Christ used the parable of the sower, to describe Himself teaching the Gospel message. Out of His four seed-sowings, only one landed in good ground and bore fruit, that is, reached people who "hear the message and retain it . . . and persist until they bear fruit." (Luke 8:15) That is a success rate of one in four.

Let us estimate, in the absence of a teacher as charismatic as Jesus, a Yoga success rate of a mere one in a thousand—that few will persevere and "persist until they bear fruit." Given even that proportion and, estimating conservatively, assuming that ten million Americans are practicing Yoga daily (it is probably closer to 20 million) – this would mean that, in a few decades, say, thirty years-- America will have a full ten thousand, powerful, Enlightened masters.

In medieval times, the Japanese monk Esai wrote an

influential pamphlet urging his countrymen to adapt Chinese Zen Buddhism as the Japanese national way of life. He titled it, "The Land of a Thousand Buddhas." (54) In years to come, America will be home to *ten thousand* Buddhas.

As average Americans, the majority of these transformed thousands will be, like the majority of Americans, of the working class. Bursting on the public scene out of nowhere, surprising everyone, in the never-ending struggle between the owners and the workers, they will be a mighty new force on the side of the workers.

* * *

Enlightenment consciousness is not always comfortable. Expanded compassion brings more sensitivity to the sufferings of the masses. A Zen Roshi wrote, "Sitting [in meditation] one develops a sensitivity after a while and one feels the pain of the world very strongly." It was said of the Tibetan saint Milarepa, "To him, existence seemed like a huge furnace where all living creatures were roasting." (55)

Enlightenment is customarily described as blissful. However, the history of mystics testifies that, in an unfavorable environment, Enlightenment is Hell.

A person who has achieved Enlightenment has lost their conventional, protective ego covering. It can be like having no skin. Gross or violent thought forms can invade the Yogi's hyper-sensitive mind. It is not snobbery that has sent mystics to often meditate in isolated, desolate places.

Sometimes it is simply self defense.

Nevertheless, if many centuries of Asian history are any guide, the Yogi will operate, in the long run, from a new position of psychic autonomy. When we reach Realization, our old ego—our old "I"--will become outmoded. Our outlook will be transformed to a profound extent. We will perceive the world in a free, unlimited way. We will, as Whitman put it, "stand nonchalant before the cosmos."

Walt Whitman was a natural *tantrika* or body mystic. He described his Enlightenment experience as "the peace and knowledge that pass all the argument of the Earth." (56) It transformed the 34 year-old, ex-editor of the Brooklyn *Eagle* into a poetic visionary. As Vivekenanda wrote, "When a man goes into *Samadhi* [superconsciousness], if he goes into it a fool, he comes out a sage . . . the man comes out enlightened, a sage, a prophet, a saint, his whole character changed, his life changed, illumined."

In *Leaves of Grass* (1855), Whitman demonstrated that his consciousness had expanded, like the telegraph medium that was the Internet of his day, to include first, the people of the American continent and, eventually, the entire world. The term, "cosmic consciousness" was coined by Whitman's first biographer to describe his state of mind. (57) Dying in 1892, he missed a chance to meet a real Yogi from the East.

For Swami Vivekenanda, the first Indian missionary, came to America in 1893. (58) He arrived in

America with little money and few contacts, a complete unknown. Nevertheless his speech--as the representative of Hinduism--was the sensation of the World's Parliament of Religion, a multi-faith, ecumenical gathering held that year in Chicago.

He spent three years in America and later England and the Continent lecturing to enthusiastic audiences. Christian missionaries had given the Western public the idea that Hindus were ignorant worshipers of idols. Vivekananda's eloquence and intelligence favorably surprised them. He gave many newspaper interviews (the Swami was "good copy") and attracted wealthy followers.

He could have stayed comfortably in the West. Instead he went back home to work for India. Vivekananda was born the son of a Calcutta lawyer. Thus he received a Western-style, college education. Nevertheless in his youth he became an ardent disciple of an illiterate, unconventional Guru, the famous Sri Ramakrishna.

After his Guru's death, Vivekananda wandered all over India. He saw at first hand the poverty and distress of the ordinary people. At the most southern tip of the sub-continent, he had an epiphany. He decided he should visit the West to demonstrate his country's spiritual knowledge but also to bring back the Western values needed by a colonized, degraded India.

When he returned to India, crowds greeted him as a hero. He became an important figure in the so-called Hindu Renaissance, the nineteenth century cultural revival that led to the twentieth century political movement that won Indian independence. Though he died when he was only 39, Vivekenanda's collected writings fill eight volumes. (59)

His first-hand experience of the misery of the Indian masses under the cruelty of British imperial rule, as well as the arrogant racism he encountered in the West, made him radically critical of Western civilization in a contemporary-sounding way.

His writings combine deep mystical insight, stirring rhetoric and clear explication. His greatest work is a commentary on the ancient *Yoga Sutras.* It is obviously written by a truly Realized Soul, yet at the same time, it is radically democratic, scientific-minded and humanist in its view.

In this great book, *Raja Yoga* (60), Swami Vivekenanda notes the paradox that religions like Christianity and Buddhism are based on the Realization experiences achieved by historic individuals—the founders. Yet the same religions then tell their followers that "the age of miracles is over." They claim that no one can equal the perceptions of a Christ or Buddha today.

"This I entirely deny," boldly asserted Swami Vivekenanda, "religion is not only based upon the experiences of ancient times . . . no man can be religious until he has the same perceptions [as the founders of religions]." The aim of making ourselves the spiritual equal of a Christ or Buddha sounds like blasphemy or fantasy to Western ears. But for Vivekenanda it is a practical, scientific goal: "Yoga is the science which teaches us how to get these [Christ-like or Buddha-like] perceptions." (61)

"Men forgot that All deities reside in the human breast," wrote Blake, *"God only Acts & Is, in existing beings or Men"* (62).

Vivekananda urged Americans to make a revolutionary turn inward. The conscious mind, he believed, is not our real, central core. It is, in reality, in contemporary terms, just another media—albeit the the first of media--between sensible reality and our central, silent, witnessing.

Like all media, our minds need to be consistently studied and understood, "studying the self to forget the self." (Dogen)

7.
REVOLUTIONARY YOGA
COUNTER CULTURE

In the opium of the people, mysticism is the active ingredient.

The blissful consciousness that the Yogi can obtain has been valued as the "highest high" by many sophisticated civilizations. The mass availability of genuine Enlightenment consciousness will present a powerful alternative to the dubious rewards of the present system. Along the path, the techniques themselves are simple, natural and enjoyable. Granted that one has half an hour a day for regular practice (not always the case), one can succeed in Yoga, that is, be completely transformed psychologically.

At that point, things will "Appear as They Are—Infinite." (Blake) (63)

The way to obtain Realization--Yoga practice--is free. This in itself is revolutionary.

Enlightenment is not for sale. You cannot buy it. You can't pay someone else to do the work for you. Starting on the meditation path, Bill Gates and the average worker are on exactly the same level. As the old hymn goes, "Nobody else can walk it for you." But with practice one can wake up to Reality just like the sages of old.

Millions of Americans now practice Yoga simply for their health. Typically, many will start Hatha Yoga just to stretch their limbs—or meditation, to relieve stress—and then get hooked. They are drawn into regular practice, or *sadhana*.

Those who make Yoga a habit and the practice part of their daily lives will eventually totally revolutionize their minds. Paradoxically it will be those who practice simply as part of their daily routine who will "stumble into" the great goal of Realization.

Then the meek shall truly inherit the earth, in their new super-consciousness. If there is one working class virtue, by necessity, it is perseverance or stick-to-it-iveness. Simple, modest souls, American working-women and men of all colors and national origins will be the ones that "persist until they bear fruit," and reach Realization.

Is it possible that you could stumble into Enlightenment without knowing what you are getting into? According to Vivekenanda, outside of India--with its virtually scientific knowledge of such transformations—that is what *always* happens. (64)

The *Matrix*-like One Dimensional Society described

by Marcuse, where "there is only one [intellectual and political] dimension and it is everywhere," (65) that co-opts into the system any attempt at rebellion--will be challenged by a radically *outside* element. That will be Asian mystical knowledge put into practice by new, working class Yogis.

They will be what in India they call "Jiva-Muktis" or Free Souls, or like the Buddhist saints of medieval India. They acquired a reputation for being as unconventional as they were uncontrollable and as Enlightened personalities for (in one scholar's words) being utterly

> unconcerned with allegiance of any variety, preferring the untrammeled Existence of a psychic world in which ritual systems, social rules, lineage concerns, scriptural continuity, and the other paraphernalia of institutional Buddhism were simply jettisoned for personal liberation. (66)

These new master rebels will be beyond society's conditioning. They will be beyond society's control. They will have lost their mental chains, their "mind-forged manacles." (Blake). Their communities will have radically different values.

Like the early Christians within the Roman Empire, they will form the core of a revolutionary, new society within the old, corrupt one.

> The [Roman] empire was hierarchial, exclusive, centralized . . . . Early Christians created an alternative, inclusive and egalitarian social organization . . . . Offering a vision and

organization for an alternative form of social interaction, the movement challenged the perception that Rome was . . . the invincible ruling power. . . . The Christians demystified it, exposed its shortcomings . . . revealed its lies and numbered its days." (67)

In one of Blake's visions, he depicts the mystic insight achieved by the Jewish prophets as enabling them to protest social injustice:

> The Prophets Isaiah and Ezekiel dined with me, and I asked them how they dared so roundly to assert that God spoke to them . . . .

> Isaiah answer'd: "I saw no God, nor heard any, in a finite organical perception; but my senses discover'd the infinite in everything, and I was then perswaded, & remain confirm'd, that the voice of honest indignation is the voice of God, I cared not for the consequences, but wrote." (68)

8.
"PARANORMAL" POWERS

An historian of world religions, Mircea Eliade, wrote of Yoga:

> In India a Yogi has always been regarded as a *mahasiddha*, a possessor of occult powers, a "magician." That this uninformed opinion is not wholly mistaken is made clear to us by the whole spiritual history of India, where the magician has always played an important part. India has never been able to forget that in certain circumstances man can become a "man-god." She has never been able to accept the prevailing human condition composed of suffering, powerlessness and precariousness. She has always believed that there are men-gods, magicians, for she has always had before her the example of the Yogis. (69)

Enlightened Americans will be surprised to discover that, like the Yogis of India, they possess so-called psychic powers. In fact, some will not realize they have reached Enlightenment until they become aware that they possess abilities such as telepathy and pre-cognition.

Enlightenment is a subjective experience. You can't tell if the person next to you has gotten Realization. What will be apparent to others will be the so-called paranormal abilities the Yogis possess. They will be the outward sign of their radically changed inward state. In India, a Yogi who has succeeded in the path is called a "saddhu" because he has mastered the "siddhis" or occult powers. (70)

Like the telescopes produced by Galileo and Newton, before they revealed their new theories, the sensation that their powers will initially create will subsequently enable the *saddhus* to get their new, revolutionary world-view before the public.

Psychic powers are not the goal in themselves. The goal is Enlightenment or Liberation. These powers are the by-product of that realization. If splitting the individual ego is like splitting the atom, and Enlightenment is like an atomic explosion, extraordinary powers are like the light and heat thrown out by the nuclear blast.

It is important to understand these seemingly miraculous powers are natural, not super-natural. That is difficult for Americans to accept. Left over from religion is the idea of a non-material soul or spirit. This is our contemporary, reactionary, philosophical context.

> The bourgeois world outlook is in the first place *conservative*, and for that reason hostile to a scientific study of human society with all its revolutionary implications. In the second place, so far as form is concerned, it is most commonly *religious*, regarding the existing order as in some

way divinely sanctioned. Even when not openly religious, it retains certain anti-scientific features, exalting "mind" or "spirit" above "mere matter." (71)

Thus, Western philosophy since before Descartes has been *dualist*, as in mind vs. matter. Americans are taught to think of spirit or consciousness as being *non*-physical. Consciousness and minds are traditionally placed in a cloudy category, different from solid, material things, called since Aristotle *meta*-physical, that is, beyond the physical.

Similarly, within each individual, religion and mainstream Western philosophy split us into two parts. As Plato says in his *Republic*:

> We may call that part of the soul whereby it reflects, rational; and the other, with which it feels hunger and thirst and is distracted by sexual passion and all the other desires, we will call irrational appetite. (72)

Or as St. Paul put it, more succinctly, "my body . . . fights against the law that my mind approves of." (Romans 7.23) Thus, we are supposed to be spiritual souls trapped in material bodies. But how can the two interact? They are two different orders of being.

Behind changeable, material things lies (in this view) an eternal, spiritual substance which is somehow more real than material reality. This eternal something may be called God or the Soul or philosophical forms or ideas.

What are the Platonic Ideas? For one of McLuhan's media-analyzing "Toronto school," the leftist scholar Eric Havelock, Plato's philosophy was produced by the shift from oral to written culture in ancient Greece--the new technology of the alphabet. Plato's thought is an example of what McLuhan termed the "Narcissus effect" of new media. New technology can "enhance yet entrance," extend but also numb or distort human consciousness.

Today we say, "If it isn't on the Net, it isn't real." In Plato's time, if it wasn't a written word, it wasn't real. Just as, in the view of contemporary idealist thinkers, such as the late Jean Baudrillard, today's electronic media spectacle is more real than physical life, so in Plato's time, the then new medium of the written word was fetishized.

To such philosophical idealists, the alphabet-created abstractions of metaphysics were more real than sensible, corporeal life. The ideas were timeless and eternal because, unlike spoken language, they were written out words. As such, they were fixed and preserved forever--in the visualized sounds of the phonetic alphabet.

From Plato onward, mainstream Western philosophy has been primarily metaphysical. By contrast, Eastern and Marxist philosophy are dialectical. As Swami Vivekananda explained:

"Thus we find these two opinions. One is that there is something behind both body and mind which is an unchangeable and immovable substance [i.e., Ideas or God or the soul]; and the other is that there is no such thing as immovability or unchangeability in the universe; it is all change and nothing but change." (73)

Marxist philosophy is the latter--*dialectical* and radically *non-dualist.* In *Capital,* Marx explained why a dialectical view is necessarily historical and critical:

> the dialectic . . . includes recognition of the existing state of things, at the same time also, the recognition of the negation of that state, of its inevitable breaking up; because it regards every historically developed social form as in fluid movement . . . it is in its essence critical and revolutionary. (74)

For the Marxist, everything is in motion and interconnected with everything else because nothing exists except matter in motion. As Engels wrote, "The real unity of the world consists in its materiality." (75) Nothing is supernatural or metaphysical. The only difference between a rock and your brain, to a Marxist, is that your brain is more complexly organized, to the point of having human consciousness. "Mind itself is merely the product of matter." (76)

Matter and mind can interact because both are the same thing. Consciousness is a material activity. (The term Altered *States* of Consciousness, popularized by the idealist minded psychologist Charles Tart, should really be Altered Consciousness *Behavior*.) To the Marxist, consciousness is a dialectical interaction between our subjective awareness and the objective world. But both are part of nature.

That is why, in the old USSR, subjects for research that would have been condemned as "para-normal" in the West were perfectly acceptable to Soviet scientists.

The psychologist's Leonid Vasiliev's 1930's experiments, using hypnotism to induce long-distance mental telepathy, would be one example. (77) In a socialist society, based on dialectical materialism, there was never any question of the results validating supernaturalism, since the experiments were carried out and interpreted, from start to finish, in a completely materialistic, naturalistic way.

In recent years, the brain experiments of neuro scientists, employing new technology, are finding evidence based, real life answers to questions concerning human perception and cognition that traditional philosophers have been batting back and forth without conclusions for centuries.

As a result of new knowledge, a new school of cognitive psychology has arisen, called the "Embodied Mind Thesis," one that recognizes our awareness as the product of the interplay of the world and our body's brain, in effect, confirming the Marxist view of consciousness.

Of course, since they are Americans, these scientists naturally speak in terms inherited from pragmatism, not Marxism. They write of our cognition as being "interactive" and "embodied," rather than dialectical and materialistic. Nevertheless. they are describing the same reality.

Two advocates of this theory, a cognitive linguist,

George P. Lakoff, and a philosopher, Mark Johnson, together wrote, of the body basis of all so-called spiritual psychological states:

> What is the locus of the real spiritual experience that people have in cultures around the world? This experience can only be embodied. It must be a consequence of what is happening in our bodies and brains. . . .

> The concept of spirituality in our culture has been defined mostly in terms of disembodiment and transcendence of this world. What is needed is an alternative conception of embodied spirituality that at least begins to do justice to what people experience. (78)

9.
DIALECTICS: MARXIST, BUDDHIST

Like Marxism, Eastern philosophy is *dialectical* and radically *non-dualist*. As a modern Buddhist explained:

The Buddha described the world as an unending flux of becoming. All is changeable continuous transformation, ceaseless mutation and a moving stream. . . . . The teaching of the impermanent nature of everything is one of the main pivots of Buddhism . . . Change is the very constituent of reality. In accepting the law of impermanency or change, the Buddha denies the existence of eternal substances. (79)

"All created things are impermanent (transitory)," were among Buddha's last words. (80) A melancholy sense of the evanescent, ephemeral nature of reality is marked in cultures influenced by Buddhism. Because all things in this world are conditioned and transient (*anicca*) they are considered to have no real independent identity (*anatta*).

Of course, many religions have lamented the swift

passing of all things in this life. As we read in Isaiah, "all flesh is grass, and all the goodliness thereof is as the flower of the field: The grass withereth, the flower fadeth." (Isaiah 40.6)

The conclusion religions usually draw is that one should turn away from the real world of change to an imaginary, religious world. "The grass withereth, the flower fadeth: but the word of our God shall stand for ever." (Isaiah 40.8) For giving up the actual world, Western religion rewards us with a consolation prize, our very own, immortal soul.

The Buddhist view is radically different. Instead of limiting the ever-changing dialectic to the physical world, Buddhism, with relentless logic, extends dialectics to include even that sanctuary granted to us by Western philosophy and religion: our very own identities. We ourselves, in the Buddhist view, are simply temporary combinations of causes and conditions.

Our egos, our souls, everything that constitutes what we think of as our Selves are equally transitory and therefore unreal. Because everything is impermanent, for most of us, life is suffering (*dukkha*). It is due to our ignorance concerning the fundamental nature of reality that we suffer: we keep trying to hold on to a world that is ever-changing.

"Time and money are both like that. Once they're gone you wonder where they went and what you did with them." (Orson Welles' *The Magnificent Ambersons*)

Buddhism offers us a practical way to end such desire-fueled suffering. By practicing Yogic mental discipline we can, with sustained effort, gradually gain control of our unruly minds and so get the upper hand over desire. "He who overcomes in this world this fierce craving . . . sorrow falls off from him." (81)

In the Buddhist view, most humans are ruled by passion. Led about by desire for what their senses show them, they are psychologically passive. "As rain breaks through an ill-roofed house, so passion makes its way into an unreflecting mind." (82)

Through Yogic meditation we can, by contrast, activate our minds. "From meditation springs wisdom." (82) "He who delights in quieting his thoughts, always reflecting . . . he will cut the bonds of death." (83)

The key is to understand that the perception of a "self" is an illusion. The self-seeking individual, ego-sense (which is so totally central to bourgeoise culture) is an illusion. As D.T. Suzuki wrote, "Buddhism finds the source of all evils and sufferings in the vulgar material conception of the ego-soul, and concentrates its entire ethical force upon the destruction of the ego-centric notions and desires." (84)

We have no sovereign intellect or immortal soul, in fact, no real, permanent identity. What we mistakenly think of as our selves are just temporary conglomerates of physical and psychological elements that are called *skhandas.*

The Marxist counterpart to the Buddhist doctrine, that there is no permanent, eternal soul, is Marx's repudiation of the idea of a permanent, unchanging human nature. Human nature, taught Marx, is simply the "ensemble of social relations." (85)

Human consciousness is a product of the material conditions of society. These conditions are constantly developing, as are their products, the ideas inside our heads. Despite the right wing delusion that one can't change human nature, in reality, as Marx pointed out in *The Poverty of Philosophy,* on the contrary, "the whole of history is nothing but a continual transformation of human nature."

Both dialectics, Buddhists and Marxists, oppose philosophical speculation for its own sake. They are practical and results oriented. They want to change the world, not just interpret it. But theory (or wisdom) is also a must. For both, theory must inform practice and practice must be theorized—they are necessarily a unity.

For the Buddhist also, there is no dualism, no split between the mind and the world. All is consciousness. In practice, this view is like the Marxist. Both affirm the unity of humankind with nature. Occultist and Marxist agree: "Thoughts are things."

Because they are the same "stuff," matter and mind can interact. Vivekananda explained that mind or consciousness and matter are equally part of nature. Therefore, both can be controlled: "Nature also includes the mind; mind is in nature; thought is in nature; from thought, down to the grossest form of matter, everything is in nature, the manifestation of nature." (86)

Compare Engel's very similar viewpoint:

We by no means rule over nature . . . like someone standing outside nature—but that we, with flesh, blood and brain, belong to nature and exist in its midst . . . The more . . . men feel, but also know, their unity with nature . . . the more impossible will become the senseless and anti-natural idea of a contradiction between mind and matter, man and nature, soul and body . . . . (87)

Matter and mind are basically the same, therefore, logically, Vivekenanda explains, "The Yogi claims that he who controls mind controls matter also." (88)

Thus Vivekenanda points to a rational, scientific explanation for the process by which the Yogi acquires seemingly supernatural powers. "When the ignorant see these powers of the Yogi, they call them miracles," he writes. (89) But the solution to the problem posed by the seeming irrationality of such powers is to understand the unity of our inner thoughts with the outer world. "They are not two different things . . . They are but two aspects of one thing . . . If then we have control of the internal [mental], it is very easy to have control of the external [physical world]." (90)

Engels wrote that the dialectical laws that govern human thought are abstracted "from the history of nature and human society." (91) The same process rules both the entire physical universe and the ideas within our own minds.

This is truly "To see the world in a grain of sand," the macrocosm within the microcosm. The whole contained in the part was a principle also demonstrated in *Capital*. Marx exposed the secret flim-flam of the whole, gigantic, capitalist system in his analysis of its smallest, atomic unit—the "cellular unit of capitalism"—a shoe, a coat, a bushel of wheat--the humble, manufactured commodity. (92)

The Buddhist equivalent to the cellular theory was the myth of Indra's Net. To illustrate the all-in-one and one-in-all interconnectivity of the universe, they imagined a net interwoven with jewels each of which--by itself--reflected all the other jewels in the vast net--as each commodity, in Marx's analysis, contains within its small self, the whole gigantic contradictions of the system.

Similarly, to the Tantras, each individual human body is a not theoretically but actually a microcosm of the entire cosmic macrocosm. It is the Tantric view that within each of us is contained the whole planet, in fact, the universe. The Tantric Buddhists maintained that, "the Buddha revealed . . . that the cosmos is contained in man's own body." (93) "It is this six foot long carcass, friend . . . that, I [Buddha] declare, lies the world, and the cause of the world and the cessation of the world." (94)

"Walt Whitman, a cosmos, of Manhattan the son" (Song of Myself).

Meditating on the nature of the dialectic, Lenin reached a paradoxical conclusion along the same lines of the Tantric Buddhist masters:

> The individual exists only in the connection that leads to the universal. The universal exists only in the individual and through the individual. Every individual is (in one way or another) a universal. Every universal is (a fragment, or an aspect, or the essence of) an individual. (95)

If the Tantrikas are correct and the universe is contained within each of us, then concludes Swami Vivekenanda, "he who has conquered the internal nature controls the whole universe." (96)

Q.: How was Jesus able to calm the waves of the Sea of Galilee?

A.: Because he had first learned to calm the waves of thoughts in his mind.

Malcolm X revealed he had reached a similar insight into human nature when he remarked, "For one to control one's thoughts and feelings means one can actually control one's atmosphere and all who walk into its sphere of influence."

10.
MIRACLE WORKERS WILL HAVE
REVOLUTIONARY EFFECTS

Paranormal powers are central to the one history book of the New Testament, the "Acts of the Apostles." It positively revels in the extraordinary magical performances of the lower-class Jesus movement. Will the Enlightened Americans of the future follow its example?

Centuries before, Buddha had urged his followers to avoid public shows of miracles. (He also made a useful distinction between mind-affecting miracles and those affecting physical objects as well.)

The author of "Acts" will have nothing of that attitude. On the contrary, the Christians' wonder-working ability were proof that, in the spiritual supermarket of the Roman Empire, non-Christian creeds were just Brand X. "Many miracles and wonders were done through the apostles, which caused everyone to be filled with awe." (Acts 2:43) When Paul returns to Christian churches after his missionary trips, his reports emphasize the magical deeds performed by himself, Peter, Philip and others.

The "signs and wonders" are proclaimed as *confirmatory*. That is, they are proof that God is backing the Christians.

Thus Peter, Paul and the other Apostles created sensations—for Christ's sake. They made the blind see and the dead rise—and they also struck people blind or dead. They held mass public healings. They provoked numerous urban riots. They carried out several magical prison breaks.

Eventually, they so awed their contemporaries with their powers that they were mistaken for gods on earth, Paul and Barnabas taken to be Hermes and Zeus, respectively. The Christians believed they were like the prophets of old of whom Hebrews 11:33 says, "Through faith they fought whole countries and won."

***

What wonderful revolutionary enthusiasm! However, what is needed today, as Vivekenanda urged, is a *non-mysterious* explanation of mysticism. "Anything that is secret and mysterious in . . . Yoga should at once be rejected," he wrote. Instead, "the science of . . . Yoga proposes to put before humanity a practical and scientifically worked out method of reaching the truth" of Liberation, which " ought to be preached in the public streets, in broad daylight." (97)

In the nineteenth century, the "utopian" socialism, which preceded Marx and Engels, was superseded by their "scientific" socialism. (98) In the twenty-first century, the old, religious, *utopian* mysticism will be made obsolete by a new, secular, *scientific* mysticism. Scientific mysticism will be open to everyone.

Religion in America will not be abolished. But it will be outmoded as the stage coach was by railroads and cars. There will be a new, surer way of reaching the psychological destination which religion once promised us. As Whitman foresaw, in his Preface to the 1855 edition of *Leaves of Grass,* someday in America the "God" idea will disappear, replaced at long last by the "common average man":

> The whole scene shifts.—The relative positions change.—Man comes forward inherent, superb,--the soul, the judge, the common average man advances ascends to place.—God disappears.—The whole idea of God, as hitherto, for reasons, presented in the religions of the world, for the thousands of past years . . . disappears—There will soon be no more priests. Their work is done. A new order shall arise, and they shall be the priests of man and every man shall be his own priest.

Similarly Blake prophesied, in "The Everlasting Gospel" a day will dawn when

> *Thou art a Man, God is no more,*
> *Thy own humanity learn to adore.*

***

In the nineteenth century, print literacy, recognized as essential to democracy, was acquired through political struggles, by the American workers. (99) Today, it is of epoch importance that a non-mysterious, secular understanding of mysticism informs our peoples' current grass-roots, democratizing spread of transforming psychic knowledge, our gaining of, so to speak, Yogi literacy.

What movement in the past would a future American Yogic counter-culture be like? The answer might lie in medieval India.

The Tantric movement was a sort of Indian Protestant Reformation. "Tantrism was a grass roots movement, whose members hailed from the castes at the bottom of the social pyramid in India, corresponding to the lower working class in our society." (100)

Tantric Yoga appeals to Americans. It is not mental, but body based. The techniques are easy and enjoyable. And they quickly yield powerful results.

The Tantras opposed the body-hatred of the priestly Brahmin elite. Tantric techniques were designed to secure Enlightenment speedily and for ordinary people. The *tantrikas* brought spiritual transformation back to earth, into a path of salvation via the body. Instead of damning sex, they controlled sexual energy to transform themselves.

Just as many do today, the *tantrikas* viewed their age of social upheaval in religious terms, as a going-to-hell "end-time." The *tantrikas* felt that society was passing through a Dark Age or "Kali Yuga." In such a time, few people are good and conditions are difficult for achieving Realization.

Thus the techniques used were made deliberately *easy*. Mantra repetition, Hatha Yoga postures and breathing exercises are fun. For couples, Tantric sex is serious fun.

Tantric techniques can be practiced by anyone. One doesn't have to learn Sanskrit or move to a monastery. Goraksha, the founder of Hatha Yoga, was so humble (legend has it) his mother found him in a shit pile. (101) The long-popular Transcendental Meditation mantras sold by the followers of Maharishi Mahesh Yogi are essentially Tantric, in their simplicity and potency.

***

What will mystic knowledge for the masses mean politically? For the first time in American history, ordinary working people will have access to powers, which have always been so assumed by their very nature to be restricted to a small elite, that they are called "occult" or secret. For the first time, the working class will become, in truth, "Miracle" Workers.

Their slogan will be: *Super Powers to the People!*

The workers' states of the East were not destroyed by armies or by bombs although they were forced to spend huge amounts to counter such threats aimed at them. In their so-called "fall"--their "being pushed" would be more accurate--the West manipulated religion and nationalism, God and country, the old standbys. (102)

But what was novel and undoubtedly crucial was the demoralizing penetration of "blue jeans and Coca-Cola," that is, subversion via Western pop culture and media consumerism. The psychological factor was decisive. It was media manipulation of the inner, subjective factor—on a mass scale--that made capitalist counter-revolution possible.

As Marshall McLuhan prophetically wrote, in the chapter of *Understanding Media* concerning "Weapons":

> Ideological warfare in the eighteenth and nineteenth centuries proceeded by persuading individuals to adopt new points of view, one at a time. Electronic persuasion by photo and movie and TV works, instead, by dunking entire populations in new imagery.

In the future, what could be more appropriate, dialectically speaking, than the workers incorporating into their own struggle the very weapon that had defeated them --the inner, psychic factor? As an old Roman proverb has it, *Fas est et ab hoste docen,* which means, "It is proper to be taught by one's enemy."

In other words, in the late twentieth century, socialist, working class power was Negated by Western, psychological-based advertising and propaganda. The twenty-first century, however, will witness the ultimate example of the dialectical law of the Negation of the Negation.

Just as the class consciousness of the workers was negated by the psychological manipulation of their psyches via electronic media, Yogic psychological knowledge and new media will in turn negate that negation--the now prevailing mass consumerism.

The mass socialist movement of the nineteenth century will return and be repeated—but on a higher level, equipped with mystical knowledge. Passive, broadcast-driven drones no more, the workers, mastering new media, will be activated to re-claim their own psyches.

As Rosa Luxemburg wrote, "Socialism in life demands a complete spiritual transformation in the masses degraded by centuries of bourgeois class rule. Social instincts in place of egotistical ones, mass initiative in place of inertia, idealism which conquers all suffering . . . ." (103)

The appearance of a growing number of morning stars or prophetic personalities will presage the coming of that epoch. With "a new way of seeing reality," Antonio Gramsci prophesied from prison, "new artists will be born from the movement." (104)

The working class wizards will be the fulfillment of Gramsci's dream of "organic intellectuals" rising from the masses, that is (from the point of view of the Establishment), from nowhere. They will help make the cultural atmosphere electric before the political lightning actually strikes.

However social change is not a matter of a few

isolated geniuses. The capitalist "hegemony" over the public mind will be defeated by the rise of a new *working class counter-culture* that will offer a better way of life to the broad masses of ordinary people.

As Gramsci wrote:

For a mass of people to be led to think coherently and in the same coherent fashion about the real present world, is a "philosophical" event far more important and "original" than the discovery by some philosophical "genius" of a truth which remains the property of a small group of intellectuals. (105)

11.
ONE BIG UNION, ONE BIG MIND

In practice, the answer to the old, philosophical riddle of identity, *who are you?* should be in the plural. In fact, the question should be *who are we?* For this is what the ancient sages meant when they said, Mind is one, or Consciousness is one.

Mental Liberation dissolves your individual consciousness in the mass, collective consciousness. It's a shift in the way you know the world, an epistemological change. When you achieve Enlightenment, it's not only an emotional or moral but a radical *perceptual* change. When you achieve Enlightenment, it's not that you love everybody. When you achieve Enlightenment, essentially you *are* everybody.

When your individual ego snaps, you will desire to "raise up the masses," because you will have *become* the masses. "This is our evolution," wrote a Tantric lama, "from an ordinary, limited and deluded person, trapped within the shell of a petty ego, into a fully evolved, totally conscious being of unlimited compassion and insight."

The Industrial Workers of the World have their slogan, "One Big Union." All the workers in America should unite in One Big Union—that is their goal.

The mystic goal is similar, in seeking to join the One Big Mind of which our limited, individual minds are each small parts. As a commentator on Hegel put it, "the greatest obstacle to the rational ordering of the world is simply that individual human beings do not realize that their minds are part of this universal mind."

Twenty-five centuries ago, Buddha taught his *Four Noble Truths*:

First: life is suffering.

Second: suffering has a cause.

Third: suffering can be ended by liberation.

Fourth: there is a method to obtain Liberation. (106)

Perhaps the unconsummated romance of the 1960s, between the angel of Asian mysticism and the devil of European revolutionary Marxism, will now finally be accomplished, the revolutionary "marriage of Heaven and Hell."

Today, with knowledge of both European Marxism and Asian psychology, we honor Buddha's achievement most genuinely by acknowledging his historical limitations and then moving beyond and overcoming them.

As to his historical limitations, the Indian Marxist critic and poet, Ram Vilas Sharma, wrote:

> Instead of focusing attention on class greed, the suffering engendered by the domination of one class over another, Buddha spoke of greed in general, suffering and misery in general and hence the path of human salvation pointed out by him is also general and was incapable of alleviating, much less removing altogether, the specific human suffering of a given social epoch. (107)

Today, with a new, revolutionary, scientific, understanding of both our inner selves and our global society, we can revise old Buddha in his own, innovative, practical spirit and specifically up-date the ancient laws.

We can formulate the *Four Working Class Truth*s:

First: life is exploitation.

Second: exploitation has a cause—the wage-slave, capitalist system.

Third: the system can be ended by Revolution.

Fourth: there is a method to achieve Revolution: Marxist Leninism + Yoga Psychology.

A Zen Roshi wrote, "The object of gaining an

insight into the inner truth of things is really to qualify oneself for greater compassionate action in the world."

Will not radical mystical insight lead to militant mass political action?

"Capitalism has triumphed all over the world but this triumph is only the prelude to the triumph of labor over capital." (Lenin) (108)

Audacious night! . . .

This is the vigil . . .

But, in the dawn . . .

We shall enter magnificent cities. (Whitman)

APPENDIX –
A WORKER'S GUIDE
TO REACHING ENLIGHTENMENT

The vulgarity of the American Yoga boom appalls many sincere spiritual seekers. In this dharmic gold rush, several thousand Yoga-related commercial trademarks have been registered. The more absurd include Snoga (Yoga on skis), Phoga (Yoga over the telephone) and Doga (Yoga for one's pet dog).

I sympathize with those objecting to such philistinism, such as the Hindu American Foundation's "Take Back Yoga" campaign. Nevertheless, does not such crass commercialization itself confirm Yoga's total Americanization?

Truly, Yoga had its origin in Hinduism. (Though I am an atheist, my own guru, Swami Muktananda, was a traditional Indian teacher.) In Asia, outside India, Buddhism was the vehicle for the spread of the meditative methods of Yoga disciplines. But most Americans today first encounter Yoga postures not in a temple but in a fitness class.

That the vehicle for spreading Yoga practices in our society is not any religion, but a physical exercise program, is unique. "Never before in the history of Yoga has the practice of physical postures assumed the importance that it has in the West." (109)

And this separation of Yoga from religion is actually a major historical development. The millions of Americans practicing Yoga have, as Marx would put it, grasped the practical kernel from the mystical flower. That is, they have grasped the inner "kernel" (of practical benefits) from Yoga, apart from its surrounding cultural context or "flower" (the beautiful Hindu religion).

(Recall our society's one previous episode of consciousness-altering activity operating apart from religion. It was the mass use of the psychedelic drug LSD. Ingesting tabs of "Acid" induced mystical experiences for millions. But the threat which LSD posed to America's Bible religions was such that its use has been violently repressed by the Federal authorities from 1966 to this time.)

The truth is, Americans do not understand the long-term results of Yoga. Many think of it as merely a path of physical development. They do not understand that, after enough years of physical exercises, both the body and the mind are transformed. As an Indian teacher explained to Americans:

"You must remember that Yoga changes the body. As you go on practicing, your body changes, it is not the same body that you had before the practice." (110)

The physical exercises change our psychological outlooks. The postures not only energize our bodies but empower our minds. As an American Yoga scholar wrote, "With sufficient practice, anyone can discover the mood-altering effects of the different *asanas* [postures], and then the real inner work will begin." (111)

After years of exercises, thousands of working people will master so-called mystical practices, which are really about turning inward and training the mind. They will attain powerful mental levels once reached only by seekers in secluded monasteries.

In 1902, the first Yogi teacher to come to the US, Swami Vivekananda, foresaw this day:

> The time is coming when these [Yogic] thoughts will be cast abroad over the whole world. Instead of living in monasteries, instead of being confined to books of philosophy to be studied only by the learned, instead of being the exclusive possession of sects and a few of the learned, they will be sown broadcast over the whole world so that they may become the common property . . . They will then permeate the atmosphere of the world and the very air that we breathe . . . . (112)

Then, as Whitman foresaw, his beloved American Democracy will provide the average woman and man not only with political liberty, and material prosperity but, more importantly, the opportunity for development, to "achieve the infinite"; the Brooklyn bard saw America as:

the best, perhaps only, fit and full means,
formulater, general caller forth, trainer, for the
millions, not for grand material personalities only,
but for immortalized souls. To be a voter with the
rest is not so much. But to become an enfranchised
man and now, impediments removed, to . . . have
the road clear'd to commence, the grand experiment
of development . . . that *is* something. (113)

Because reaching Enlightenment takes a long time,
this development lies, not years but decades in the future.

But have no doubt: this Yoga Cultural Revolution is
taking place, with major social results. Within our present
society, a mighty, Yoga counter-culture will arise, for
which the psychedelic-based, revolutionary counter-culture
of the 1960's will prove to have been a mere dress
rehearsal. And the Occupy movement, smashed by violence
temporarily, was the first harbinger of that change in
consciousness.

***

In the meantime, as regards learning Yoga practice,
one can take a correct, revolutionary attitude or a deluded,
bourgeois view. Here's what I mean:

Middle class people enjoy spending a lot of money
on expensive Yoga classes, outfits and equipment. They
like to follow incredibly successful businessmen/
"teachers."

Unfortunately, these teachers' heated-up and over-strenuous trademarked Yoga regimes are going to give the attorneys of their middle class students a lot of lucrative work, years from now, suing them for the serious spinal injuries their work-outs are causing. (114)

Alas, capitalism teaches bourgeois Americans to always compete. If the guy next to them in Yoga class knows a dozen postures, they will insist on learning two dozen. They don't want to hear that, in Yoga, "no pain, no gain" is not the operative cliché but rather, "easy does it." They, so to speak, want to go out in the field and make the plant grow faster by yanking it up from the roots.

Americans, in their ever-striving, Faustian (or Captain Ahab-like) way, have forgotten the quiet wisdom expressed in the mysterious Parable of the Growing Seed:

> Jesus went on to say: "the kingdom of God is like a man who scatters seed in his field. He sleeps at night, is up and about during the day, and all the while the seeds are sprouting and growing. Yet he does not know how it happens. The soil itself makes the plants grow and bear fruit." (Mark 4: 26-28)

The Hindu Swami Vivekananda's thoughts read like a gloss on this Christian parable:

> The plant grows of itself. So it is in regard to the spiritual growth of every man. None can teach you; none can make a spiritual man [or woman] of you. You have to teach yourself; your growth must come from inside. (115)

Working class people might think they can't afford to learn Yoga. For instruction can indeed be expensive. Some Yoga teachers in New York are paid $150 an hour. A membership in a East Side Yoga "studio" runs about $1500 for one year. The same business charges $23--for a single walk-in class--plus "Mat Rental $2." (116)

But working class people should not be intimidated. It does not require money to succeed in Yoga. One imagines there are rich youths today wasting their inheritances on Yoga teachers and classes and outfits and equipment the way their forefathers wasted the family fortune on the more traditional cocaine and call girls. But working people should reap the benefits of these ancient practices more intelligently.

Contrary to what you have been told by the Yoga industry--

First, most Yoga classes are a waste of time and money. You will always tend to be distracted by the other students. They will want to socialize or compete with you. With the same effort, you will make greater progress in a quiet corner of your own room. There you can learn to concentrate. This is the advice of many realized souls.

Guatama Buddha left his companions and successfully sought Awakening by himself. In the *Bhagavada Gita,* Krishna teaches the true seeker to "concentrate his mind, remaining in solitude and alone" (Chapter VI, verse 10). Similarly, Jesus taught, "when you pray, go to your room and close the door." (Matthew 6:6)

Second, buying Yoga equipment is a waste of money. Buy a twenty-dollar Yoga mat, if you must. Or you can just fold over a blanket on which to perform your *hatha* Yoga postures. Your initial stiffness will give way with time. Don't strive for heroic eight-hour sessions. Instead, make a habit of a half-hour routine of basic postures.

After your physical stretching and breathing, sit in meditation. Select a pillow or a small cushion you find comfortable. Sit before a candle and a picture you find inspiring and perhaps light a stick of incense. With these few, inexpensive items, you will be fully equipped to reach the highest degree of mystical insight.

Third, these days, to pay Yoga teachers is not necessary. Every public library has a half dozen books and DVDs illustrating the postures and breathing exercises. Study them. While doing your routine, learn to listen to your *own* body. Your own practice is your best instructor. As Swami Sivananda wrote,

"Within you is the Teacher of teachers." (117)

How-to manuals aside, the best book on Yoga for Americans is *Raja Yoga* by Swami Vivekananda. If you think Yoga is just an exercise routine, you will learn from that book that it is more. It is a path of psychological liberation. Toward this goal, the Swami provides guidance that is not other-worldly or mysterious but rather "a practical and scientifically worked-out method." (118)

With time, Yoga dissolves the false personality

imposed on you by society. As a scholar of Yoga wrote:

> Yoga is a frontal attack on the fixed patterns of
> thinking and feeling acquired in the course of one's
> life. It aims at emancipating . . . one's psyche by
> scraping off layer after layer of false identification .
> . . Yoga means a systematic pursuit of self-
> realisation leading to the recovery of the Self . . .
> (George Feuerstein) (119)

Finally, persist. Those who succeed will be those
who make the practice a regular, routine habit. Human
personality, as Behaviorists and Buddhists both understand,
is simply a bundle of such habits. If you can give Yoga an
hour or even a half-hour every day, eventually you WILL
reach Enlightenment. But think in terms of decades—not a
weekend workshop.

As Jack Kerouac wrote, "Walking on water wasn't
built in a day."

NOTES

1 - Susan Moran, "Meditate on This: Yoga Is Big Business," *The New York Times*, December 28, 2006.

2 - Edward Conze, *Buddhism, Its Essence and Development* (New York: Harper & Row, 1971), p. 103.

3 - Georg Feuerstein, *Sacred Paths, Essays on Wisdom, Love and Mystical Realization* (New York: Larson Publications, 1991), p. 142.

4 - S. Radhakrishnan, "The Dhammapada," in Sarvepalli Radhakrishnan and Charles A. Moore, eds., *A Sourcebook in Indian Philosophy* (Princeton University Press, Princeton, New Jersey 1957), p. 325.

5 - Albert Weller, "Esai's Promotion of Zen for the Protection of the Country," in George J. Tanabe, *Religions of Japan in Practice* (Princeton, New Jersey: Princeton University Press 1999), p. 66.

6 – Raymond Williams, *George Orwell* (New York:

Columbia University Press, 1971), p. 86.

7 - F.V Konstantinov, ed., *The Fundamentals of Marxist-Leninist Philosophy* (Moscow: Progress Publishers, 1982, 1979), pp. 101-109.

8 - Evelyn Underhill, *Mysticism, A study in the nature and development of Man's spiritual consciousness* (New York: New American Library, 1974), p. 421.

9 – Karl Marx, *Capital*, I (New York: International Publishers, 1967), p. 20.

10 - Kenneth Ch'en, *Buddhism in China, A Historical Survey* (Princeton, NJ: Princeton University Press, 1964), p. 350.

11 - Debiprasad Chattopadhyaya, *Indian Philosophy, A Popular Introduction* (New Delhi: People's Publishing House, 1964), p. 124.

12 – Frederick Engels, *Origin of the Family, Private Property and the State* (New York: International Publishers, no date), p. 135.

13 - Nicholas Ostler, *Empires of the Word: A Language History of the World* (New York: Harper Collins, 2005), p. 34.

14 – Marshall McLuhan, *Understanding Media: The Extensions of Man* (New York: McGraw-Hill Book Company, 1964), pp. 82-83.

15 - Ostler, p. 208.

16 - K. Sri Dhammananda, *What Buddhists Believe* (Taipei, Taiwan: The Corporate Body of the Buddha Educational Foundation, 1993), p. 5.

17 - Rev. Siridhamma, *The Life of the Buddha* (Kuala Lumpur, Malaysia: Buddhist Missionary Society, 1983), p. 73.

18 - Chattopadhyaya, p. 124.

19 - V.I. Lenin, *What Is To Be Done? Burning Questions of Our Movement* (New York: International Publishers, 1969, c. 1902), p. 21.

20 - Lenin, pp. 149-175.

21 - Lenin, p. 78.

22 - Richard A. Gard, ed., *Buddhism* (New York: Washington Square Press Book, 1963), p. 155.

23 - Chattopadhyaya, p. 127.

24 - Radhakrishnan and Moore, p. 325.

25 - Hellmuth Hecker, "Buddhist Women at the Time of The Buddha," *The Wheel* (Kandy, India 1982), downloaded from
        http://www.accessto
insight.org/lib/authors/hecker/wheel292 html.

26 - Arthur F. Wright, *Buddhism in Chinese History* (Stanford, CA: Stanford University Press, 1959), p. 17.

27 - Ch'en, p. 224.

28 - Wright, p. 60.

29 - Ch'en, p. 148.

30 - Ch'en, p. 249.

31 – Harold A. Innis, *The Bias of Communication* (Toronto: University of Toronto Press, 2006), pgs. 18, 50.

32 - Noble Ross Reat, *Buddhism: A History* (Fremont, CA: Jain Publishing Company, 1994), p. 144.

33 – Debiprosad Chattopadhyaya, "Some Problems of Early Buddhism," in Rahul Sankrityayan, *et al,, Buddhism, The Marxist Approach* (New Delhi: People's Publishing House, 1970), p. 15.

34 - Lionel Landry, "Migrations of Buddhism," *AskAsia.org,* website downloaded from http://www.askasia.org/teachers/essays/essay.php?no=23.

35 - Stuart Sovatsky, quoted by Nora Isaacs, "Yoga Is More Than Just Showing Up, But That Does Help," *The New York Times,* September 9, 2007.

36 - Wright, p. 98.

37 – Karl Marx, "A Contribution to Critique of Hegel's *Philosophy of Right,"* in *Karl Marx, Early Writings,* T. B.

Bottomore, ed.(New York: McGraw Hill Book Company, 1963), p. 52.

38 - "Transcendental Meditation – Is TM a Religion?" *Behind the TM Facade* website downloaded from http://www.behind-the-tm-façade.org/transcendental_meditation-religion.htm# legal.

39 - "Scientific Research on TRANSCENDENTAL MEDITATION and TM-SIDHI Programs," website downloaded from http://www.maharishi.org/ tm/research/hime.html.

40 - Stewart J. Lawrence, "Yoga's Christian Army," *Counter Punch,* December 25, 2013.

41 - David J. Stewart, "Kundalini, the Mother Power," downloaded from
http://www.jesus-is-savior.com/
False%20Religions/New%20Age/kundalini.htm.

42 - Radhakrishnan and Moore, p. 298.

43 - James L. McClain, *Japan, a Modern History* (New York: W. W. Norton & Company, 2002), p. 175.

44 - Sri Swami Sivananda, *Kundalini Yoga* (Teri-Garhwal, U.P, India: Divine Life Society, 1991), p. 193.

45 - Frederic W. Grannis, M.D., "History of Cigarette Smoking and Lung Cancer," downloaded from
http://www.smokinglungs.com/cighist.htm.

46 - Sivananda, p. 151.

47 - Vivekenanda, "Raja Yoga," in *Complete Works,* I (Kolkata, India: Advaita Ashrama, 2003), p. 405.

48 - Norman Mailer, *The Armies of the Night: history as a novel: the novel as history* (New York: Penguin Books, 1968), pp. 120-125.

49 ˙ Morris Dickstein, *The Gates of Eden, American Culture in the Sixties* (New York: Basic Books, Inc., 1977), p. 12.

50 – Susan Moran, "Meditate on This: Yoga Is Big Business," New York *Times*, December 28, 2006.

51 - Sivananda, p. 187.

52 - Engels, p. 145.

53 – A Commission of the Central Committee of the C.P.S.U.(B.), eds. *History of the Communist Party of the Soviet Union (Bolsheviks), The Short Course* (New York: International Publishers, 1939), p. 129.

54 – George J. Tanabe, *Religions of Japan In Practice* (Princeton: Princeton University Press, 1999), p. 66.

55 - Sivananda, p. 135.

56 - Whitman, "Song of Myself," *Leaves of Grass and Selected Prose* (New York: Modern Library, 1950), p. 27.

57 - Richard Maurice Bucke, *Cosmic Consciousness, a Study in the Evolution of the Human Mind* (New York:

Penguin Books, 1999).

58 - Wilhem Halbfass, *India and Europe, An Essay in Understanding* (Albany, New York: State University of New York Press, 1988, 1981), pp. 228-242.

59 - Swami Vivekenanda, *Complete Works,* I-VIII, (Kolkata, India: Advaita Ashrama, 2003).

60 - Vivekenanda, I, pp. 119-315.

61 - Vivekenanda, I, p. 123.

62 – William Blake, "The Marriage of Heaven and Hell," in *The Portable Blake* (New York: The Viking Press, 1968), p. 259.

63 - Blake, p. 258.

64 - Vivekenanda, 'Raja Yoga,' *Complete Works,* I, pp. 183-184.

65 - Herbert Marcuse, *One Dimensional Man* (London: Sphere Books, Ltd., 1968), p. 26.

66 - Ronald M. Davidson, *Indian Esoteric Buddhism, A Social History of the Tantric Movement* (New York: Columbia University Press, 2006), p. 190.

67 - Warren Carter, "The Roman Empire Challenged by the Early Christians," in A. Blasi, ed., *Handbook of Early Christianity, Social Science Approaches* (Walnut Creek, CA: Altamira Press 2002), p. 455.

68 - Blake, p. 256.

69 –Mircea Eliade, *Patanjali and Yoga* (New York: Schocken Books, 1975), p. 103.

70 - David Snellgrove, *Indo-Tibetan Buddhism, Indian Buddhists and Their Tibetan Successors* (Boston. MA: Shambhala Publications Inc., 2002), p. 148.

71 - David Guest, *A Textbook of Dialectical Materialism* (New York: International Publishers, 1939), pp. 18-19.

72 – Plato, *Republic,* F.M. Cornford, trans. (New York: Oxford University Press 1973), p. 137.

73 –Vivekenanda, "The Real and the Apparent Man," *Complete Works,* II, p. 273.

74 - Marx, *Capital*, I, p. 20.

75 - Engels, quoted in T. Vlasova, *Marxist-Leninist Philosophy: Diagrams, tables, illustrations for students of Marxist-Leninist theory* (Moscow: Progress Publishers, 1987), p. 32.

76 - Engels, in Vlasova, p. 42.

77 - Leonid Vasiliev, *Mysterious Phenomena of the Human Psyche* (New Hyde Park, New York), 1965.

78 - George Lakoff and Mark Johnson, *Philosophy in the Flesh, The Embodied Mind and Its Challenge to Western Thought* (New York: Basic Books, 1999), p. 564

79 – K. Sri Dhammananda, p. 86.

80 - Rev. Siridhamma, *The Life of the Buddha* (Kuala Lumpur, Malaysia: Buddhist Missionary Society, 1983), p. 87.

81 - "Dhammapada," Radhakrishnan and Moore, p. 318.

82 - Radhakrishnan and Moore, p. 313.

83 - Radhakrishnan and Moore, p. 293.

84 - D. T. Suzuki, *Outline of Mahayana Buddhism* (New York: Schoken Books, 1977), p. 146.

85 – Karl Marx, "Theses On Feuerbach," in Marx and Frederick Engels, *The German Ideology* (New York, International Publishers 1991), p. 121.

86 - Vivekenanda, I, p. 210.

87 - Frederick Engels, *Dialectics of Nature* (New York: International Publishers, 1979), p. 293.

88 - Vivekenanda, I. p. 257.

89 - Vivekenanda, I. p. 148.

90 - Vivekenanda, I, pp. 257-8.

91 - Engels, *Dialectics of Nature*, p. 26.

92 - Marx, *Capital,* I, pp. 71-83.

93 - Mircea Eliade, *Yoga, Immortality and Freedom* (Princeton, New Jersey: Princeton University Press, 1973), p. 204.

94 - Eliade, p. 179.

95 - Lenin, "On the Question of Dialectics," *Collected Work*, XXXVIII (Moscow: Progress Publishers, n.d.), p. 359.

96 - Vivekenanda, I, p. 257.

97 - Vivekenanda, p. 134.

98 - Friedrich Engels, *Socialism: Utopian and Scientific* (New York: International Publishers), 1982.

99 - "The Struggle for Public Schools," Digital History Website downloaded from www.digitalhistory.uh.edu/dis_textbook.cfmsmtID=2&psid 3535

100 - Feuerstein, p. 141.

101 - Feuerstein, p. 132.

102 - Sean Gervasi, "The Destabilization of the Soviet Union," *Covert Action Quarterly,* Number 35, Fall 1990.

103 - Rosa Luxemburg, "The Russian Revolution," in Peter Hudis and Kevin B. Anderson, eds., *The Rosa Luxemburg Reader* (New York: Monthly Review Press, 2004), p. 306.

104 - Gramsci, in David Forgacs, *An Antonio Gramsci Reader, Selected Writings 1918-1934* (New York: Schoken Books, 1988), p. 393.

105 - Gramsci, in Forgacs, p. 327.

106 - Gard, pp. 93-123.

107 - Ram Vilas Sharma, "Some Aspects of the Teaching of Buddha," in Sankrityayan, p. 57.

108 - V. I. Lenin, "The Three Component Parts of Marxism," in Selsam and Martel, *Reader in Marxist Philosophy From the Writings of Marx, Engels and Lenin* (New York: International Publishers, 1963), p. 40.

109 - Anne Cushman, "The New Yoga," *Yoga Journal,* March 29, 2005.

110 - Vivekananda, I, p. 224.

111 - George Feuerstein, *Yoga, the Technology of Ecstasy* (Los Angeles: JP Tarcher, 1989), p. 189.

112 - Vivekananda, "The Real and the Apparent Man," *Complete Works* II, p. 288.

113 - Whitman, p. 476.

114 - William J. Broad, "How Yoga Can Wreck Your Body," *New York Times Magazine,* January 8, 2012.

115 - Vivekananda, "The Ideal of a Universal Religion," *Complete Works* II, p. 385.

116 - *Schedules & Information,* New York Yoga, June 2009.

117 - Swami Sivananda, *Sadhana* (Tehri-Garhwal, U.P., India: Divine Life Society, 1993), p. 677.

118 - Vivekananda, I, p. 128.

119 - George Feuerstein, *Introduction to the Bhagavad Gita, Its Philosophy and Cultural Setting,* (Wheaton, Ill.: The Theosophical Publishing House, 1983), p. 128.

Michael R McBrearty, received shaktipat (initiation) from Swami Muktananda. He was, for some years, on the staff of the Reference Center for Marxist Studies. He has earned a B.F.A. from New York University and an M.F.A. from Columbia University. He lives in Manhattan.

As of this writing, he can be reached at
mmcb15@earthlink.net